Skills Scope & Sequence

Week	1	2	3	4	5	6	7	8	9	10	11	12	13	14	15	16	17	18	19	20	21	22	23	24	25	26	27	28	29	30	31	32	33	34	35	36
Numbers and Operations																																				
write number sentences	●	●	●	●	●		●	●			●	●	●		●		●				●	●	●		●	●	●	●	●	●				●	●	
write word problems					●		●						●				●								●		●		●							
read & write numbers	●	●	●	●	●	●	●	●	●	●	●	●	●	●	●	●	●	●	●	●	●	●	●	●	●	●	●	●	●	●	●	●	●	●	●	●
read & write number words	●	●	●	●	●	●	●			●	●	●	●	●	●	●	●	●	●	●	●	●		●	●	●	●	●	●	●	●	●	●	●	●	●
count by twos, fives, tens	●	●	●	●	●	●	●			●	●	●	●	●	●	●	●	●	●	●	●	●		●	●	●	●	●	●	●	●	●	●	●	●	●
odd/even									●					●					●		●				●				●					●		
ordinal numbers		●				●				●				●				●				●				●				●				●		
estimation			●				●								●				●					●			●	●			●				●	
greater/less than, equal to			●	●		●	●	●	●	●	●				●	●			●		●			●			●	●			●	●				●
properties, number relationships	●		●	●		●	●			●		●	●		●	●	●	●	●	●	●	●	●	●	●	●	●	●	●	●	●	●	●	●	●	●
fractions			●		●		●					●			●	●			●	●			●			●		●			●	●				●
tens and ones								●															●													
money	●	●							●	●			●	●				●			●	●		●	●		●		●		●	●	●	●		●
addition facts	●	●	●	●	●	●	●	●	●	●	●	●	●		●	●	●	●	●	●	●	●		●	●	●	●	●	●	●	●	●	●	●	●	●
subtraction facts	●	●	●	●	●	●	●	●	●	●	●	●	●	●	●	●	●	●	●	●	●	●		●	●	●	●	●	●	●	●	●	●	●	●	●
column addition			●	●	●	●	●	●	●	●	●	●	●	●	●	●	●	●	●	●	●	●		●	●	●	●	●	●	●	●	●	●	●	●	●
2-digit addition and subtraction			●		●				●			●	●		●						●			●			●				●	●				●
3-digit addition & subtraction									●												●				●				●		●	●				
solve word problems	●	●	●	●	●	●	●	●	●	●	●	●	●	●	●	●	●	●	●	●	●	●	●	●	●	●	●	●	●	●	●	●	●	●	●	●

Week	1	2	3	4	5	6	7	8	9	10	11	12	13	14	15	16	17	18	19	20	21	22	23	24	25	26	27	28	29	30	31	32	33	34	35	36
Algebra																																				
sort and classify	●	●		●	●	●		●	●	●			●				●		●		●	●	●		●	●			●	●			●			●
name, extend, create patterns	●		●	●	●		●	●	●			●	●		●	●				●	●		●	●	●		●	●			●	●	●		●	●
Geometry																																				
shapes	●	●	●	●	●	●	●	●	●	●	●	●	●	●	●	●	●	●	●	●	●	●	●		●	●	●	●	●		●	●	●	●	●	●
symmetry			●				●				●				●				●			●	●				●				●				●	
directions about location																										●									●	
Measurement																																				
weight, length, & capacity		●				●				●				●	●		●	●	●		●	●				●			●	●				●		
time	●	●		●		●		●		●		●		●		●				●		●		●				●		●		●		●		●
Data Analysis and Probability																																				
read and interpret graphs	●						●				●				●		●		●					●				●				●		●		
create graphs																																●	●	●		
use tally marks				●								●				●				●				●				●				●				
sort by common attributes																		●							●											

4

What's in
Daily Math Practice

36 Weekly Sections

Monday through Thursday

- two computation problems

- two items that practice a variety of math skills

- one word problem

Friday

Friday's format includes one problem that is more extensive and may require multiple steps. These problems emphasize reasoning and communication in mathematics.

Also featured on Friday is a graph form where students record the number of problems they got correct each day that week.

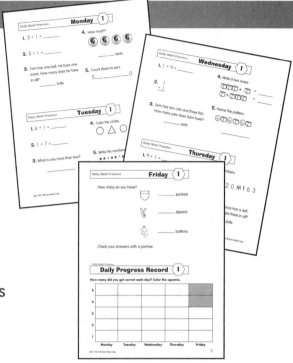

Additional Features

Scope and Sequence

Scope and sequence charts on pages 3 and 4 detail the specific skills to be practiced and show when they will be presented. The skills included are found in math texts at this level.

Answer Key

The answer key begins on page 117.

How to Solve Word Problems Chart

Award Certificate

How to Use *Daily Math Practice*

You may want to use all of the following presentations throughout the year to keep each lesson fresh and interesting.

1. Make overhead transparencies of the lessons. Present each lesson as an oral activity with the entire class. Write answers and make corrections using an erasable marker.

   As the class becomes more familiar with *Daily Math Practice*, you may want students to mark their answers first and then check them against correct responses marked on the transparency.

2. Reproduce the pages for individuals or partners to work on independently. Check answers as a group, using an overhead transparency to model the correct answers. (Use these pages as independent practice only after much oral group experience with the lessons.)

3. Occasionally you may want to use a day's or even a full week's lesson(s) as a test to see how individuals are progressing in their acquisition of skills.

Some Important Considerations

1. Allow students to use whatever tools they need to solve problems. Some students will choose to use manipulatives, while others will want to make drawings.

2. It is important that students be able to share their solutions. This modeling of a variety of problem-solving techniques provides a great learning benefit. Don't scrimp on the amount of time you allow for discussing how solutions were reached.

Suggestions and Options

1. Sometimes you will not have taught a given skill before it appears in a lesson. These items should then be done together. Tell the class that you are going to work on a skill they have not yet been taught. Use the practice time to conduct a minilesson on that skill.

2. Customize the daily lessons to the needs of your class.

   • If there are skills that are not included in the grade-level expectancies of the particular program you teach, you may choose to skip those items.

   • If you feel your class needs more practice than is provided, add these "extras" on your own in the form of a one-item warm-up or posttest.

  EMC 750 • © Evan-Moor Corp.

Monday ⟨ **1** ⟩

1. 3 + 1 = _____

2. 5 + 1 = _____

3. Tom has one ball. He buys one more. How many does he have in all?

_____ balls

4. How much?

_____ cents

5. Count down to zero.

5 _____ _____ _____ _____ 0

Tuesday ⟨ **1** ⟩

1. 6 + 1 = _____

2. 1 + 7 = _____

3. What is one more than two?

_____

4. Color the circles.

◯ △ ◯ ▢ ◯

5. Write the numbers.

★★ + ★★ = ★★★★

_____ + _____ = _____

Wednesday 1

1. $1 + 4 =$ _____

2. $\begin{array}{r} 1 \\ + 1 \\ \hline \end{array}$

3. Sam has two cats and three fish. How many pets does Sam have?

_____ pets

4. Write it two ways:

$\square\square\square + \square$ = _____

$\square + \square\square\square$ = _____

5. Name the pattern.

_____

Thursday 1

1. $9 + 1 =$ _____

2. $1 + 2 =$ _____

3. $8 + 0 =$ _____

4. Circle the numbers.

4 7 a 9 2 0 M f 6 3

5. Ann has a doll. Tricia has a doll. How many dolls are there in all?

_____ dolls

How many do you have?

     _____ pockets

     _____ zippers

     _____ buttons

Check your answers with a partner.

Daily Progress Record 〈 1 〉

How many did you get correct each day? Color the squares.

	Monday	Tuesday	Wednesday	Thursday	Friday
5					
4					
3					
2					
1					

1. Which is heavier?

2.
$$\begin{array}{r} 2 \\ + \ 2 \\ \hline \end{array}$$

3. Color the first one.

4.
$$\begin{array}{r} 4 \\ + \ 2 \\ \hline \end{array}$$

5. How much?

_____ cents

1. 6 + 2 = _____

2. 2 + 1 = _____

3. This is a triangle. △

　　　yes　　no

4. Are there enough?

　　yes　　no

5. The bike rack is full. It has four big bikes and two little bikes. How many bikes are there in all?

_____ bikes

1. 2 + 7 = _____

2. 3 + 2 = _____

3. Color the ones with four wheels.

4. Write the time.

| 8:00 |

_____ o'clock

5. Write the numbers.

5 10 ___ ___ ___

1. 8 + 2 = _____

2. 5 + 2 = _____

3. Write the numbers.

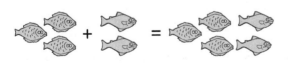

____ + ____ = ____

4. Mrs. Brown has two new pairs of shoes. How many new shoes does she have?

_____ shoes

5. What comes next?

△ △ ○ △ △ ___

Friday ⟨2⟩

How many played each game?

swings _____

balls _____

ropes _____

climbing bars _____

Which one is the most?

_____

Recess Games	
swings	🧍🧍🧍🧍
balls	🧍🧍🧍🧍🧍🧍🧍🧍
ropes	🧍🧍🧍
climbing bars	🧍🧍🧍🧍🧍

🧍 = 1 child

Daily Progress Record ⟨2⟩

How many did you get correct each day? Color the squares.

	Monday	Tuesday	Wednesday	Thursday	Friday
5					
4					
3					
2					
1					

1. 3 + 5 = _____

2. 4 + 3 = _____

3. Write the number.

 one _____

two _____

three _____

4. Write = to show if they are the same.

⊘ ⊘ ☐ ⊘ ⊘

⊘ ⊘ ⊘ ⊘ ☐ ⊘ ⊘ ⊘ ⊘ ⊘

⊘ ☐ ⊘

5. The dog had one bone. He found one more bone. How many bones did he have altogether?

_____ bones

1.   3
      + 3
     _____

2. ☐ How many sides? _____

How many corners? _____

3. Mom put five cookies on the plate. Mia ate one. How many were left?

_____ cookies

4.   7
      + 3
     _____

5. Write the numbers.

____ + ____ = ____ + ____

Wednesday 3

1. 2 + 3 = _____

2. | + | + | = _____

3. Estimate.

2   12   100

4. Two birds were in the nest. One flew away. How many were left?

_____ bird

5. Write the numbers.

_____

_____

_____

Thursday 3

1. Color $\frac{1}{2}$ of the ball.

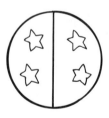

2. Write the numbers.

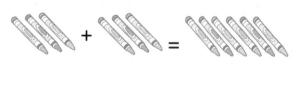

____ + ____ = ____

3.   3
       + 8

4.   6
       + 3

5. The train has a 🚃 , a 🚃 , and two 🚃 🚃 . How many cars does it have in all?

_____ cars

12   EMC 750 • © Evan-Moor Corp.

Friday ⟨3⟩

Color a pattern.

Tell about the pattern.

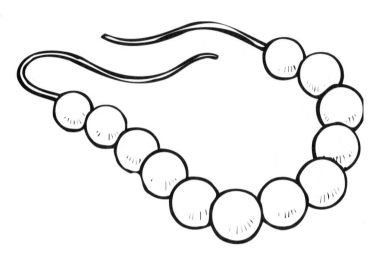

Daily Progress Record ⟨3⟩

How many did you get correct each day? Color the squares.

	Monday	Tuesday	Wednesday	Thursday	Friday
5					
4					
3					
2					
1					

1. 4 + 5 = _____

2. 2 + 4 = _____

3. What comes next?

 _____

4. Make one line for each flower.

5. Mary has two , one , and one . How many altogether?

_____

1. 4 + 4 = _____

2. 4 + 6 = _____

3. One little 🐱, two little 🐱🐱, three little 🐱🐱🐱.

How many kittens in all?

_____ kittens

4. Write the time.

_____ o'clock

5. Write the number.

six _____ eight _____

seven _____ nine _____

1. $4 + 3 =$ _____

2. $4 + 7 =$ _____

3. Color the square blue. Color the circle red. Color the triangle yellow.

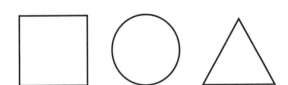

4. Bob put two cherries in the bowl.

$0 + 2 =$ _____

Bob ate two cherries.

$2 - 2 =$ _____

5. Luis had two green hats and three red hats. How many hats in all?

_____ hats

---

1. $1 + 8 =$ _____

2. $\begin{array}{r} 8 \\ + 4 \\ \hline \end{array}$

3. Rita had four big beads and two little beads. How many beads altogether?

_____ beads

4. Write the numbers.

 $= ?$

____ $+$ ____ $=$ ____

5.

   yes   no

    yes   no

    yes   no

Friday 〈4〉

Put the animals in two groups. Draw a red line around the animals in one group. Draw a blue line around the animals in the other group.
Tell about the groups.

Daily Progress Record 〈4〉

How many did you get correct each day? Color the squares.

	Monday	Tuesday	Wednesday	Thursday	Friday
5					
4					
3					
2					
1					

1. $5 - 1 =$ _____

2. $7 - 1 =$ _____

3. Think.

What is $3 + 3$? _____

4. How much?

_____ cents

5. How many stamps?

_____ stamps

1. $2 + 4 =$ _____

2. $9 - 1 =$ _____

3. Count down.

10 ___ ___ ___ ___ ___

___ ___ ___ ___ 0

4. $3 + 2 = 5$ yes   no

$2 + 3 = 5$ yes   no

$5 + 2 = 3$ yes   no

5. Sally ate two carrots, one apple, and four grapes. How many things did she eat?

_____ things

Wednesday ⟨5⟩

1. $9 - 3 =$ _____

2. $5 + 5 =$ _____
$3 + 3 =$ _____
$2 + 2 =$ _____

3. There were ten in the bed and one rolled out. How many were left? _____

4. Mark the pattern.

ABAB   AABAAB

What shape comes next?

_____

5. Write the numbers.

_____ + _____ = _____

Thursday ⟨5⟩

1. $10, 11, 12,$ _____,
_____, _____, 16

2. 4
    -1
   _____

3. Mr. Black has five fish.
Mr. Brown has seven fish.
Who has more fish?

_____

4. 6
    -1
   _____

5. $4 + 0 = 4$ yes   no
$0 + 4 = 4$ yes   no
$4 + 4 = 0$ yes   no

Number to put the balls in order.

How many did you get correct each day? Color the squares.

	Monday	Tuesday	Wednesday	Thursday	Friday
5					
4					
3					
2					
1					

1. 5 − 2 = _____

2. 4 + 3 = _____

3. Mark has two pennies. His mom gives him three more pennies. How many pennies does he have?

_____ pennies

4. What time is it?

○ 1 o'clock

○ 10 o'clock

○ 11 o'clock

5. Mark the second hat.

1. 8 − 2 = _____

2. 2 − 2 = _____

3. Draw a triangle.

How many sides? _____
How many corners? _____

4. Which is heavier?

5. Sean has three letters. If he needs a stamp for each letter, how many stamps does he need?

_____ stamps

1. 7 – 2 = _____

2. 5 + 3 = _____

3. Tell how many petals.

_____

_____

_____

_____

4. Mark the square buttons with two holes.

    ○

○   ○

5. There were two red fish and five blue fish. How many fish were there in all?

_____ fish

---

1. 6 – 2 = _____

2. 4 + 5 = _____

3. Ron read six pages today and four pages yesterday. How many more pages did he read today?

_____ pages

4. Mark the number sentence that tells about the picture.

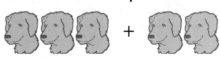

○ 3 + 2 = 6   ○ 3 + 3 = 6

○ 3 + 2 = 5   ○ 3 – 2 = 5

5. 3 + 1 – 1 = _____

Friday ⟨6⟩

Thomas has 3 parrots, 2 canaries, and 1 macaw.
How many birds does he have?

_____ birds

If he can keep 2 birds in a cage, how many
cages does he need?

_____ cages

Daily Progress Record ⟨6⟩

How many did you get correct each day? Color the squares.

5				
4				
3				
2				
1				
Monday	**Tuesday**	**Wednesday**	**Thursday**	**Friday**

Monday ⟨7⟩

1. $5 - 3 =$ _____

2. $3 + 6 =$ _____

3. There were six eggs in the box. Two eggs broke. How many are left?

_____ eggs

4.

Mark the half.

○   ○

5. Write a story problem to go with the numbers. $2 + 1 = ?$

_____

_____

_____

Tuesday ⟨7⟩

1. $8 - 3 =$ _____

2. $4 + 3 =$ _____

3. $5 = 5$ yes no
$5 = 6$ yes no
$5 = 4$ yes no

4. Finish the pattern.

5. There are two red beads and two blue beads and two green beads. How many beads in all?

_____ beads

1. 3 – 3 = _____

2. 1 + 6 = _____

3. Estimate.

○ 200   ○ 20   ○ 2,000

4. 4 + 2 = 2 + 4   yes   no

    5 + 2 = 2 + 4   yes   no

5.  +

Write a number sentence to tell how many.

_____

---

1. 9 – 3 = _____

2. 7 – 3 = _____

3. Write the numbers.

ten   _____

five   _____

seven   _____

4. Mark the squares

5. If Tommy found three big feathers and three little feathers, how many feathers did he find in all?

_____ feathers

Mrs. Watson's class made a weather graph.
Read the graph and answer the questions.

How many rainy days?   _____

How many cloudy days?   _____

Were there more rainy and cloudy days
together than sunny days?

yes   no

Write something else you know from
reading the graph.

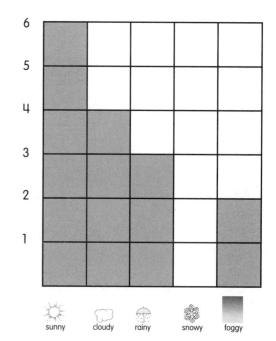

sunny   cloudy   rainy   snowy   foggy

Daily Math Practice

Daily Progress Record ⟨7⟩

How many did you get correct each day? Color the squares.

	Monday	Tuesday	Wednesday	Thursday	Friday
5					
4					
3					
2					
1					

1. 3 + 7 = _____

2. 6
   – 4
   _____

3. Each glass needs one cup of milk.
   How much milk for six glasses?

   _____ cups

4. Tally to show how many.

_____ ten   _____ ones

5. Finish the pattern.

 _____ _____

1. 8 – 4 = _____

2. 6
   + 3
   _____

3. There are five frogs on the log.
   If two frogs jump off, how many
   are left?

   _____ frogs

4. Mark the time.

   ○ 12:00   ○ 8:00
   ○ 9:00   ○ 6:00

5. Write the numbers.

   two + three + four = nine

   _____ + _____ + _____ = _____

1. $10 + 10 =$ _____

2. $\begin{array}{r} 9 \\ -\ 4 \\ \hline \end{array}$

3. 5 boys and 5 girls went up the steps. How many went up?

_____

4. Count by twos.

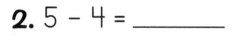

___ ___ ___ ___ ___

5. $4 = 4$ yes   no

$4 < 4$ yes   no

$4 > 4$ yes   no

1. $7 - 4 =$ _____

2. $5 - 4 =$ _____

3. There were 25 students in Mrs. White's class. One new student came. How many are in Mrs. White's class now?

_____ students

4. Mark the triangles.

○   ○ ◤

○ ▲   ○ ■

5. Write a number sentence.

 + =

____ + ____ = ____

Friday ⬡8

Zoo Math

 How many ears do six elephants have? _____ ears

 How many feet do four zebras have? _____ feet

 How many tails do three monkeys have? _____ tails

Tell how you know.

Daily Progress Record ⬡8

How many did you get correct each day? Color the squares.

	Monday	Tuesday	Wednesday	Thursday	Friday
5					▓
4					▓
3					
2					
1					

28   EMC 750 • © Evan-Moor Corp.

1. $9 - 5 =$ _____

2. $4 + 6 =$ _____

3. Wes has two bags of candy. Each bag has 6 pieces. How much candy does Wes have altogether?

_____ pieces

4. Are the teams even? yes   no

5. How much?

_____ cents

1. $8 - 5 =$ _____

2. $\begin{array}{r} 4 \\ + 5 \\ \hline \end{array}$

3. There are five eggs in the nest. If one breaks, how many are left?

_____ eggs

4. Count backward.

20 19 ___ ___

___ ___ ___ ___

5. How many tens?

_____ tens

Wednesday 9

1. $3 + 3 + 2 = $ _____

2. $9 - 6 = $ _____

3. Mary's coat has three pockets on each side and one in the back. How many pockets does it have?

_____ pockets

4. $3 + 4 = 7$ yes   no

    $4 - 7 = 3$ yes   no

    $4 + 3 = 7$ yes   no

    $7 - 3 = 4$ yes   no

5. A square has three equal sides.

    yes   no

Thursday 9

1. $10 - 4 = $ _____

2. $7 + 2 = $ _____

3. Josh has three beanbag babies and Todd has four.

Who has more? _____

How many more? _____

4. Mark the pattern.

ABAB   AABAAB   ABBABB

5. $322 + 0 = $ _____

Friday ⟨9⟩

Write your name in two different patterns.

Name the patterns that you used.

Examples: PEtePEtePEte   PeTePeTe

1. [   ]

2. [   ]

Daily Progress Record ⟨9⟩

How many did you get correct each day? Color the squares.

	Monday	Tuesday	Wednesday	Thursday	Friday
5					
4					
3					
2					
1					

1. $12 - 2 =$ _____

2.
$$
\begin{array}{r}
5 \\
3 \\
+\ 1 \\
\hline
\end{array}
$$

3. The pumpkin vine had six pumpkins. Bob picked two. How many were left?

_____ pumpkins

4. Mark the third bird.

5. $4 + 2 = 6$ yes no

$3 + 3 = 6$ yes no

$6 + 0 = 6$ yes no

$5 + 2 = 6$ yes no

1. $10 - 7 =$ _____

2. $8 + 3 =$ _____

3. Jenny picked up two pennies. She put them with her other six pennies. How many pennies does Jenny have?

_____ pennies

4. Mark the hats that have stripes and bills.

5. Write the time.

_____ o'clock

Wednesday ⟨10⟩

1. 5 + 2 + 4 = _____

2.   7
      – 1
   ——

3. Sue had a double scoop of ice cream. Tom had a triple scoop. Who had the smallest amount?

_____

4. How many petals?

_____   _____

_____   _____

5. Which weighs more?

○

○

Thursday ⟨10⟩

1. 9 – 8 = _____

2. 9 – 7 = _____

3. Tommy had 10 cents. He bought a pencil for 5 cents. How much does he have left?

_____ cents

4. Mark the squares.

   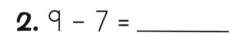

5. Four cherries and five grapes equal _____ pieces of fruit.

Friday ⟨10⟩

Solve this problem.

$$10 - 5 + 6 - 1 + 4 - 2 = \underline{\hspace{2cm}}$$

Daily Math Practice

Daily Progress Record ⟨10⟩

How many did you get correct each day? Color the squares.

	Monday	Tuesday	Wednesday	Thursday	Friday
5					▓
4					▓
3					▓
2					▓
1					

1. $5 + 4 =$ _____

2. $7 - 2 =$ _____

3. Juan ate four tortillas for lunch and four tortillas for supper. How many did he eat?

_____ tortillas

4. Write the number.

eight _____

six _____

three _____

zero _____

5. $10 + 10 + 10 + 10 =$ ___

---

1. $8 + 3 =$ _____

2. $3 + 2 + 3 =$ _____

3. I put six sea stars, three snails, and a sunfish into a pail. How many are in the pail?

_____

4. Color $\frac{1}{2}$.

5. $5 + 4 = 4 + 5$

yes   no

$6 + 4 = 4 + 5$

yes   no

Wednesday ⟨11⟩

1. $0 + 9 =$ _____

2. $2 + 6 =$ _____

3. $10 = 5 + 4$ yes   no

   $10 < 5 + 4$ yes   no

   $10 > 5 + 4$ yes   no

4. Draw three circles.
Color one blue. Color two red.

Write a number sentence to tell about the circles.

____ + ____ = ____

5. Five boys, five girls, and one dog = _____ members on the team.

Thursday ⟨11⟩

1. $45 + 3 =$ _____

2. $17 - 5 =$ _____

3. Three girls each had three bears.
How many bears in all?

_____ bears

4. Estimate.

○ 2   ○ 24   ○ 240

5. Write four number sentences using 4, 2, and 6.

____ + ____ = ____

____ + ____ = ____

____ − ____ = ____

____ − ____ = ____

Friday ⟨11⟩

The boys and girls in Mrs. Timm's class write their names on a tooth when they lose a tooth. Here are the teeth lost in August, September, October, November, and December.

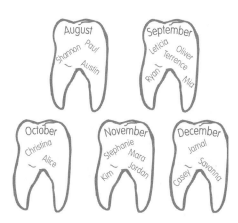

How many teeth have been lost altogether? _____

During which month were the most teeth lost? _____

During which month were the fewest teeth lost? _____

Write something else you learned by reading the graph.

Daily Progress Record ⟨11⟩

How many did you get correct each day? Color the squares.

	Monday	Tuesday	Wednesday	Thursday	Friday
5					
4					
3					
2					
1					

1. 4
    + 3

2. 7
    – 4

3. Mr. Smith sold two sacks of oranges. If each sack has eight oranges, how many oranges did he sell altogether?

_____ oranges

4. Write the time.

_____ o'clock

5. Use tally marks to show how many.

🍎 🍎 🍎 🍎 🍎 🍎

🍎 🍎 🍎

🍎 🍎 🍎 🍎 🍎

1. 6 + 6 = _____

2. 30 + 20 = _____

3. There were two raisins on each cookie. How many raisins were there on three cookies?

_____ raisins

4. Finish the pattern.

2 2 1 2 2 1 ___ ___

___ ___ ___ ___

5. Count the eyes.

👁 👁 👁 👁 👁 👁 👁 👁 👁 👁

___ ___ ___ ___ ___

EMC 750 • © Evan-Moor Corp.

1. 7 + 1 = _____

2. 54 + 1 = _____

3. There are two peanuts in each shell. How many peanuts are in six shells?

_____ peanuts

4. Mark the spheres.

5. Add two.

5 + 2 = _____

Then subtract two.

_____ – 2 = _____

1. 4 + 3 + 2 + 1 = _____

2. 13 – 7 = _____

3. The class read two books every day. How many books did they read in five days?

_____ books

4. Write the numbers.

seven _____

six _____

ten _____

two _____

5. Color $\frac{1}{4}$.

Friday ⟨12⟩

Sally went to the store. She bought four apples, six oranges, and five bananas. She ate one apple. How many pieces of fruit does she have now?

_____ pieces

Daily Math Practice

Daily Progress Record ⟨12⟩

How many did you get correct each day? Color the squares.

	Monday	Tuesday	Wednesday	Thursday	Friday
5					
4					
3					
2					
1					

EMC 750 • © Evan-Moor Corp.

1. $0 + 0 =$ _____

2. $2 + 8 =$ _____

3. Carl rode his bike two blocks to the park and two blocks home. How far did he ride?

_____ blocks

4. Mark the pattern.

t t w t t w t t w

○ abab   ○ aabaab   ○ abbabb

5. How much?

_____ cents

1. Think. $0 + 15 =$ _____

2. $2 + 9 =$ _____

3. $\begin{array}{r} 3 \\ + 4 \\ \hline \end{array}$

4. Mark the circles.

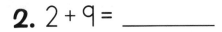

5. Brett and Bonnie ate pizza for lunch. They each had four pieces. How much pizza did they eat altogether?

_____ pieces

1. $6 + 4 =$ _____

2. $4 - 3 =$ _____

3. $1 + 5 = 6$ yes   no
$5 + 1 = 6$ yes   no
$6 + 1 = 5$ yes   no

4. Write words for the problem.

_____

_____

_____

5. Now write numbers for the problem.

____ – ____ = ____

---

1. $1 + 5 =$ _____

2. $4 - 2 =$ _____

3. Seline put three cookies and two brownies in the box for her grandma. How many treats will Grandma have?

_____ treats

4. Is it odd or even?

   odd   even

   odd   even

   odd   even

5. Mark the names for 7.

$5 + 2$ $4 + 4$ $6 + 1$

$9 - 2$ $3 + 5$ $7 + 0$

EMC 750 • © Evan-Moor Corp.

Friday ⟨13⟩

Mark needs two new tires for his bike.
If each tire costs $10, how much will he
have to spend?

$_____

Daily Progress Record ⟨13⟩

How many did you get correct each day? Color the squares.

	Monday	Tuesday	Wednesday	Thursday	Friday
5					
4					
3					
2					
1					

1. $3 + 9 =$ _____

2. $4 + 1 =$ _____

3. Sammy found two nickels in his pocket. How much did he find?

_____ cents

4. Mark the seventh bird.

5. 5 10 15 ___ ___

---

1. $2 + 5 =$ _____

2. $\begin{array}{r} 5 \\ + 6 \\ \hline \end{array}$

3. Which is heavier?

10 pounds　　100 pounds

4. Write the time.

_____ o'clock

5. There were six flowers in the vase. Two of the flowers were roses. How many other flowers were there?

_____ other flowers

1. 5 + 6 = _____

2. 7 + 4 = _____

3. Trina had three rings, two necklaces, and four bracelets. How many pieces of jewelry did she have in all?

_____ pieces

4. Draw a rectangle.

_____ sides _____ corners

5. 4 + 8 = 12   yes   no

12 + 4 = 8   yes   no

8 + 4 = 12   yes   no

1. 7 – 5 = _____

2. 4 + 8 = _____

3. Five pairs of ants marched up the hill. How many ants were there?

_____ ants

4. Mark the names for nine.

○ 3 + 6   ○ 4 + 5   ○ 2 + 7

○ 1 + 7   ○ 0 + 9

5. How much?

_____ cents

Friday ⟨14⟩

How many toes?

_____ toes

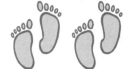

_____ toes

_____ toes

How many toes do 5 babies have?   _____ toes

Daily Progress Record ⟨14⟩

How many did you get correct each day? Color the squares.

	Monday	Tuesday	Wednesday	Thursday	Friday
5					
4					
3					
2					
1					

1. $5 + 7 =$ _____

2. $10 - 3 =$ _____

3. There were two goldfish and four red fish in the bowl. How many fish were there in all?

_____ fish

4. Are the two sides the same?

     yes   no

     yes   no

5. Finish the pattern.

---

1. $5 + 8 =$ _____

2. $4 - 4 =$ _____

3. The bag had ten cookies. If Eli ate two and Mollie ate one, how many are left?

_____ cookies

4. Mark the pizza divided in half.

5. Write the number word.

10 _____ _____ _____

1. $7 + 5 = $ _____

2. $4 + 2 + 1 = $ _____

3. Bingo hid four bones in the garden and two bones in the park. How many bones did he hide?

_____ bones

4. Estimate.

Paper Clips

5   15   50

5. $9 < 3$

yes   no

1.   4
      + 9
      ___

2.   8
      + 1
      ___

3. Four trucks and six cars were stopped at the light. How many were stopped?

_____

4. Use these numbers to write four number sentences: 3 5 8

____ + ____ = ____

____ + ____ = ____

____ − ____ = ____

____ − ____ = ____

5. Are both sides the same?

yes   no

Friday 15

         = 1 birthday

How many people have birthdays in March? _____

How many fewer people have birthdays in January? _____

Do more people have birthdays in February and April together than in January?

    yes   no

Write a number sentence to show your answer. _____

Do more people have birthdays in January and February together than in March?

    yes   no

Daily Progress Record 15

How many did you get correct each day? Color the squares.

	Monday	Tuesday	Wednesday	Thursday	Friday
5					
4					
3					
2					
1					

1. $6 + 8 =$ _____

2. $8 + 6 =$ _____

3. Deana is 11. Her sister is 6. How much older is Deana?

_____ years older

4. Which is $\frac{1}{4}$?

○

○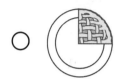

5. What comes next?

2 4 6 ____

1. $7 + 7 =$ _____

2. $7 - 7 =$ _____

3. Tony swam four laps of freestyle and six laps of backstroke. How many laps did he swim?

_____ laps

4. Finish the pattern.

____ ____ ____

5. Tally to show 12.

50

1. $7 - 6 =$ _____

2. $9 + 3 =$ _____

3. There were seven sharp pencils and two broken pencils. How many pencils in all?

_____ pencils

4. If $53 + 4 = 57$, then $57 - 4 =$ ____

5. Write the number word.

3

____ ____ ____ ____ ____

1. $6 + 9 =$ _____

2. $10 - 2 =$ _____

3. Petey hit three balls. Ann hit four balls. Terri didn't get a hit. How many hits were there?

_____ hits

4. What time is it?

_____ o'clock

5. Mark the big square.

Friday ⬡16

On Monday, four girls checked out three books each.

On Tuesday, two of the girls returned their books.

How many books are still out?

_____ books

Daily Progress Record ⬡16

How many did you get correct each day? Color the squares.

	Monday	Tuesday	Wednesday	Thursday	Friday
5					
4					
3					
2					
1					

1. $7 + 8 =$ _____

2. $9 + 2 =$ _____

3. Two polar bears walked across the ice. Six others joined them. How many bears were there in all?

_____ bears

4. 35 34 33 ___ ___

___ ___ ___ ___

___

5. Use these numbers to write four number sentences:

6   5   11

___ + ___ = ___

___ + ___ = ___

___ – ___ = ___

___ – ___ = ___

1. $8 + 7 =$ _____

2. $9 + 5 =$ _____

3. If five drummers each need two drumsticks, how many drumsticks do they need altogether?

_____ drumsticks

4. Think.

$3 + 3 + 3 =$ _____

5. Write a story to tell about the fish.

_____

_____

_____

1. 9 + 7 = _____

2. 9 – 2 = _____

3. Juanita asked for three cupcakes. She gave one to Felix and two to the twins. How many did she have left?

_____ cupcakes

4. 10, 20, 30, ____, ____,

____, ____, ____, ____, ____

5. Count the sides.

 _____

 _____

 _____

---

1. 8 + 5 = _____

2. 2 + 10 = _____

3. The hungry caterpillar ate three leaves, two strawberries, and five grapes. How many things did it eat?

_____ things

4. Tell the rule.

Group 1

 _____

_____

_____

Group 2

 _____

_____

_____

5. If 34 + 7 = 41,

then 41 – ____ = 34

Friday ⟨17⟩

Measure your chair using your shoe. Draw a picture to show your results.

Daily Progress Record ⟨17⟩

How many did you get correct each day? Color the squares.

	Monday	Tuesday	Wednesday	Thursday	Friday
5					▓
4					▓
3					▓
2					▓
1					

1. 7 + 9 = _____

2. 9 + 6 = _____

3. Which is heavier?

2 grams   20 grams

4. Mark the seventh bead.

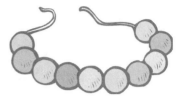

5. Lilly drew five hearts. She colored two of them red. She colored the rest pink. How many are pink?

_____ pink hearts

1. 10
+ 0

2. If 17 − 5 = 12,
then 12 + 5 = ____

3. Which thing does <u>not</u> belong with the others?

4. What time is it?

_____ o'clock

5. Mickey invited seven friends to his party. Two couldn't come. How many will be there?

_____ friends

1. $9 + 8 =$ _____

2. $5 + 10 =$ _____

3. David bought two apples for $1. How much would four apples cost?

   $ _____

4. Write the numbers.

   ___ – ___ = ___

5. 5 ___ 15 ___ 25 ___
   35 ___

1. $5 + 9 =$ _____

2. $8 - 7 =$ _____

3. Four bees flew to three flowers. How many more bees are there than flowers?

   _____ more

4. Tell the difference between a triangle and a square.

   A square has _____ sides.

   A triangle has _____ sides.

5. Mark the names for five.

   $3 + 2$ $6 - 1$ $4 + 2$
   $5 + 0$ $4 - 1$

Friday 18

How many squares are there altogether?

_____ squares

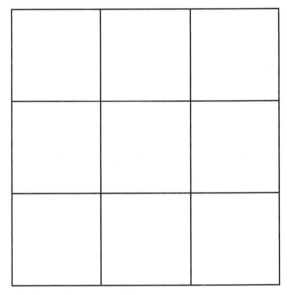

Daily Progress Record 18

How many did you get correct each day? Color the squares.

	Monday	Tuesday	Wednesday	Thursday	Friday
5					
4					
3					
2					
1					

Monday ⟨19⟩

1. $9 + 9 =$ _____

2. $6 - 3 =$ _____

3. Six girls formed two equal teams. How many girls were on each team?

_____ girls

4. If $36 + 42 = 78$, then $42 + \underline{\ \ \ } = 78$

5. Color $\frac{1}{2}$.

Tuesday ⟨19⟩

1. $6 + 5 =$ _____

2. $8 - 6 =$ _____

3. Carolina planted three rows of tulips. Each row had six bulbs. How many bulbs did she plant altogether?

_____ bulbs

4. Write a story.

_____

_____

_____

5. What is 10 more than 20?

_____

Wednesday ⟨19⟩

1. $9 + 4 =$ _____

2. $2 + 6 =$ _____

3. Chris needed four chairs. She borrowed two from Syd and two from Pam. How many more does she need?

_____ more

4. $4 = 5$ yes   no

    $4 < 5$ yes   no

    $4 > 5$ yes   no

5. Estimate.

1 pound   10 pounds   100 pounds

Thursday ⟨19⟩

1. $8 - 1 =$ _____

2. $10 - 5 =$ _____

3. Mrs. Smith checked out five books to Brad and three books to Thomas. How many books did she check out?

_____ books

4. Color the squares red.
Color the rectangles yellow.

5. Are both sides the same?

yes   no

Friday 〈19〉

Which pet is the most favorite? _____

Which pet is the least favorite? _____

Which pets were picked by the same number of children? _____

Write something else you learned by reading the graph.

My Favorite Pet

dog	🐶	🐶	🐶	🐶	🐶	🐶	🐶
cat	🐱	🐱	🐱				
mouse	🐭	🐭					
bird	🐦	🐦	🐦				
hamster	🐹	🐹	🐹	🐹	🐹		
snake	🐍						

Daily Progress Record 〈19〉

How many did you get correct each day? Color the squares.

	Monday	Tuesday	Wednesday	Thursday	Friday
5					▨
4					▨
3					
2					
1					

1. 3 – 2 = _____

2. 6 + 10 = _____

3. Beatrice put three candies on each gingerbread cookie. If she made ten cookies, how many candies did she use?

_____ candies

4. Color $\frac{1}{4}$.

5. Write the number words.

1 _____

2 _____

3 _____

4 _____

1. 4 + 8 = _____

2. 7 – 4 = _____

3. Finish the pattern.

____ ____ ____

4. Tally to show 14.

5. The bus had fifteen passengers. Four got off at the first stop. Two got off at the second stop. How many are left?

_____ passengers

1. $2 + 9 =$ _____

2. $\begin{array}{r} 8 \\ -6 \\ \hline \end{array}$

3. Bob piled the blocks in stacks of five. He had six stacks. How many blocks did he use altogether?

_____ blocks

4. 2 ___ 6 ___ 10 ___ 14 ___

5. Mark the cone.

---

1. $100 + 4 =$ _____

2. $\begin{array}{r} 5 \\ 1 \\ +2 \\ \hline \end{array}$

3. Six hats were in the lost and found. The first-graders claimed three. How many were left?

_____ left

4. Write the time.

_____ o'clock

5. If $20 + 30 = 50$, then $50 -$ ___ $= 20$

Friday ⬡20

Doug went fishing with 12 worms in his bait can and 3 in his pocket. He put a new worm on the hook every time he cast. How many times did he cast if he has 4 worms left?

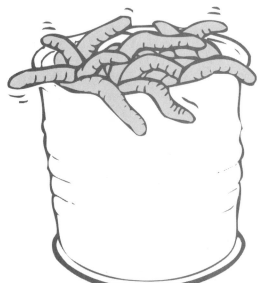

_____ times

Daily Math Practice

Daily Progress Record ⬡20

How many did you get correct each day? Color the squares.

	Monday	Tuesday	Wednesday	Thursday	Friday
5					
4					
3					
2					
1					

1. 7 + 10 = _____

2. 6 – 5 = _____

3. Rick collected two bags of cans. Joe collected three bags of cans. How many bags did they collect?

_____ bags

4. Mark the closed figures.

5. Write four number sentences using 6, 2, and 8.

_____ + _____ = _____

_____ + _____ = _____

_____ – _____ = _____

_____ – _____ = _____

---

1. 6 + 7 = _____

2. 3 + 8 + 2 = _____

3. Bill walked four blocks to Sam's house, and then he walked home. How many blocks did he walk in all?

_____ blocks

4. Name the pattern.

_____

5. 1 ten = _____

2 tens = _____

3 tens = _____

4 tens = _____

5 tens = _____

1. $647 + 0 =$ _____

2. $7 + 6 =$ _____

3. Which is longer?

4. $7 + 3 = 10,$

   so _____ – _____ = 7

5. Write the number sentence and solve the problem.

   Tom put three pears, four oranges, and one apple in the bowl. How many pieces of fruit are in the bowl?

   _____

1. $8 + 9 =$ _____

2. $10 - 6 =$ _____

3. Terry has two bikes and a wagon. How many wheels does Terry have altogether?

   _____ wheels

4. How much?

   _____ cents

5. Five is an odd number.

   yes   no

Friday 〈21〉

The cook will use one cup of cheese for each pizza. Each package of cheese holds four cups. The class ordered eight pizzas. How many packages of cheese will the cook need?

_____ packages

Daily Progress Record 〈21〉

How many did you get correct each day? Color the squares.

	Monday	Tuesday	Wednesday	Thursday	Friday
5					
4					
3					
2					
1					

1. $0 - 0 =$ _____

2. The ball box had two basketballs, three tennis balls, five soccer balls, and one super ball. How many balls in all?

_____ balls

3. $10 + 1 =$ _____
$10 + 2 =$ _____
$10 + 3 =$ _____

4. Write the time.

_____ o'clock

5. Mark the heaviest.

1. $9 + 3 =$ _____

2. $3 - 1 =$ _____

3. If five days in every week are school days, how many are at-home days?

_____ days

4. If $6 + 7 = 13$,
then $13 -$ ___ $= 6$

5. 20 ___ 30 ___ 40 ___
50 ___ 60

1. $10 + 6 =$ _____

2. $7 - 7 =$ _____

3. Chuck planted four trees. One tree died, so he planted another. How many trees did he plant?

_____ trees

4. How much?

_____ cents

5. Mark the names for 8.

$5 + 3$ $2 + 7$

$4 + 4$ $8 + 0$

$6 + 1$

---

1. $4 + 7 + 3 =$ _____

2. Fred and Gary took five boxes to the recycling center. The man paid them $1. How much money should each boy get? _____

3. The fourth mitten is striped.

   yes   no

4. $10 - 0 =$ ___

$10 - 1 =$ ___

$10 - 2 =$ ___

$10 - 3 =$ ___

$10 - 4 =$ ___

5. Mark the straight lines.

Yvonne built this stack of blocks.

It is symmetrical.

Which drawing shows how it looks from

the side?

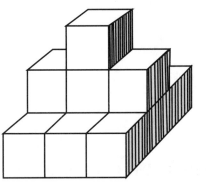

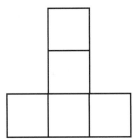 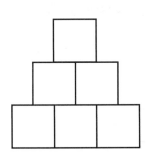 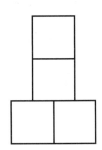

Daily Math Practice

Daily Progress Record 〈22〉

How many did you get correct each day? Color the squares.

	Monday	Tuesday	Wednesday	Thursday	Friday
5					
4					
3					
2					
1					

1. $10 + 8 =$ _____

2. $8 - 0 =$ _____

3. Three birds each laid three eggs. How many eggs are there?

_____ eggs

4. Color $\frac{1}{2}$.

5. Write the number.

zero _____ four _____

eight _____ two _____

1.
$$6$$
$$+\ 7$$

2. Penny gives her dog a bone every morning and every night. How many bones does she need in one week?

_____ bones

3. Draw a line of symmetry.

4.

____ tens + ____ ones = ____ in all

5. Write the number word.

3 _____

5 _____

7 _____

1. $9 + 7 =$ _____

2. $7 - 3 =$ _____

3. The nurse saw 4 boys with colds and 6 girls with colds. How many children did she see in all?

_____ children

4. Finish the pattern.

_____   _____

5. Mark the rectangles.

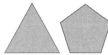

1. $15 - 6 =$ _____

2. $2 + 7 + 4 =$ _____

3. Anabel has four pink jelly beans and five purple jelly beans. If she eats three jelly beans, how many will she have left?

_____ jelly beans

4. $9 + 10 =$ _____

$10 + 10 =$ _____

5. Write four number sentences using 8, 2, and 6.

_____ + _____ = _____

_____ + _____ = _____

_____ − _____ = _____

_____ − _____ = _____

Friday ⟨23⟩

Paper Punches

Draw to show what each paper will look like when it is unfolded.

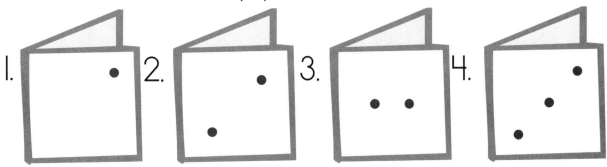

1. 2. 3. 4.

Daily Progress Record ⟨23⟩

How many did you get correct each day? Color the squares.

	Monday	Tuesday	Wednesday	Thursday	Friday
5					
4					
3					
2					
1					

Monday 24

1. $7 + 4 =$ _____

2. $14 - 8 =$ _____

3. $34 > 31$

   yes   no

4. Color $\frac{1}{4}$.

5. One octopus and two divers are in the water. How many legs altogether?

_____ legs

Tuesday 24

1. $10 + 7 =$ _____

2. $18 - 9 =$ _____

3. The truck holds ten crates, and the driver has loaded six. How many more does he need for a full load?

_____ more crates

4. Tally to show 17.

5.

one more	one less	ten more	ten less
41 ____	____ 21	6 ____	____ 39
86 ____	____ 54	30 ____	____ 97

1. 9 + 8 = _____

2. 8 – 3 = _____

3. Todd has three pencils, four markers, and twenty-two crayons in his drawing box. How many drawing tools does he have?

_____ drawing tools

4. Write the time.

_____ o'clock

5. 23 + 5 = 28, so
28 – ___ = 23

---

1. 7 + 7 = _____

2. 8 – 5 = _____

3. Two frogs ate six flies. If each frog ate the same number of flies, how many did each frog eat?

_____ flies

4. 69 < 50

yes   no

5. Finish the pattern.
0 3 0 3 0 3 ____ ____ ____

Friday 24

Each group planted ten seeds. If each seed can make one sprout, how many nonsprouting seeds did each group have?

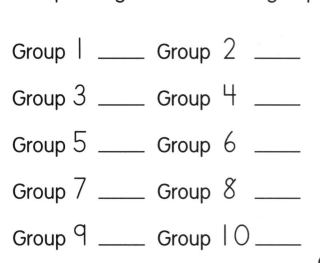

Group 1 _____ Group 2 _____

Group 3 _____ Group 4 _____

Group 5 _____ Group 6 _____

Group 7 _____ Group 8 _____

Group 9 _____ Group 10 _____

Our Seeds Sprouted

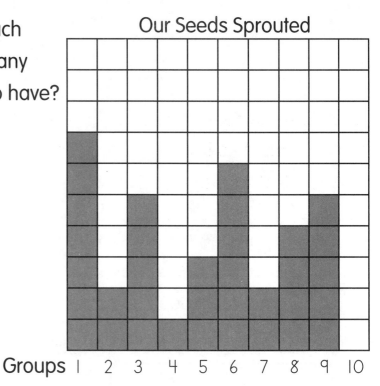

Groups 1 2 3 4 5 6 7 8 9 10

Daily Progress Record 24

How many did you get correct each day? Color the squares.

	Monday	Tuesday	Wednesday	Thursday	Friday
5					
4					
3					
2					
1					

1.
$$9$$
$$- 5$$

2. Luke needs 4 nails for each board. He has two boards. How many nails does he need?

_____ nails

3.
$$6$$
$$+ 5$$

4. How much?

_____ cents

5. 65 64 63 ___ ___

___ ___ ___

1. Think.

$2 + 4 - 2 + 1 =$ _____

2. Name the pattern.

T T s r T T s r

_____

3. $5 + 23 = 28$, so

$23 + 5 =$ ___

4. Mark the circles.

5. There were six books on the table, three books on the chair, and ten books on the shelf. How many books in all?

_____ books

1. 3 + 7 = _____

2. 12 − 3 = _____

3. 8,247 + 0 = _____

4. Write a number sentence.

____ + ____ = ____

5. 6 is an odd number.

     yes   no

1. 17 − 9 = _____

2.
$$\begin{array}{r} 7 \\ 6 \\ + 4 \\ \hline \end{array}$$

3. Scott put six books, three pencils, and a notebook in his backpack. How many things are in the backpack? _____ things

4. Write a story.   3 + 2 = 5

_____

_____

_____

5. How long is the gum?

| 1 | 2 | 3 | 4 |

_____ centimeters

What does <u>not</u> belong? Make an **X** on it.

Tell how the other things are alike.

_____

_____

Daily Progress Record 〈25〉

How many did you get correct each day? Color the squares.

	Monday	Tuesday	Wednesday	Thursday	Friday
5					
4					
3					
2					
1					

1. $9 + 10 =$ _____

2. $16 - 8 =$ _____

3. The ship had four red flags, seven green flags, and three yellow flags. How many flags were there on the ship?

_____ flags

4. Mark the second star.

5. 20 ___ ___ 35 ___ 45 ___

1. $8 + 5 =$ _____

2. $9 + 6 =$ _____

3. Each lunch bag has two sandwiches in it. How many sandwiches are in six lunch bags?

_____ sandwiches

4. Mark the heaviest.

5. Tell the rule: > or <

Group A 1, 4, 3, 6, 2, 5

All the numbers are ____ 7.

Group B 8, 10, 9, 11, 13, 12

All the numbers are ____ 7.

EMC 750 • © Evan-Moor Corp.

1. $13 - 4 = $ _____

2. $41 + 8 = $ ___, so

___ $- 8 = 41$

3. The ladder had 18 rungs. Tom climbed halfway up. How many rungs did he climb?

_____ rungs

4. $2 + 10 = $ _____

$3 + 10 = $ _____

$4 + 10 = $ _____

5. Color the circle green. Color the triangle black. Color the square pink.

1. $17 - 8 = $ _____

2. $10 + 9 = $ _____

3. Color $\frac{1}{3}$.

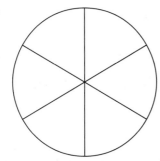

4. Five boys and seven girls stood in line. Write a number sentence about the line.

___ $+$ ___ $=$ ___

5. Mark the names for 9.

$8 + 1$ $\quad$ $7 - 2$ $\quad$ $3 + 6$

$5 + 4$ $\quad$ $0 - 9$

The soccer team scored four goals in their first game, five goals in the next game, and two goals in their third game. How many goals did they score in all?

_____ goals

If they lost their third game, how many goals did the other team have to score?

_____ goals

How many did you get correct each day? Color the squares.

	Monday	Tuesday	Wednesday	Thursday	Friday
5					
4					
3					
2					
1					

82   EMC 750 • © Evan-Moor Corp.

1. $8 + 4 =$ _____

2. $6 + 8 =$ _____

3. Tommy has three yellow cars, seven green cars, and six white cars. How many cars does he have?

_____ cars

4. Start at the star. Where is the ball?

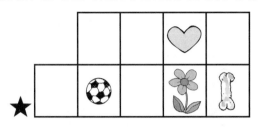

right 4 boxes   right 5 boxes

left 2 boxes   right 2 boxes

5. Write the number word.

10 _____

5 _____

7 _____

1. $7 + 3 =$ _____

2. $12 - 7 =$ _____

3. Harry caught two ants, three crickets, and six beetles. How many bugs did he catch?

_____ bugs

4. $8 < 18$

yes   no

5. Estimate.

6   12   18

Wednesday 27

1. $6 + 9 =$ _____

2. $20 - 10 =$ _____

3. Tim took four cookies. If he ate half, how many did he eat?

_____ cookies

4. Write a story problem.

$6 - 2 = ?$

_____

_____

_____

5. $23 + 21 =$ ___ + ___

Thursday 27

1. $7 + 8 =$ _____

2. $17 - 8 =$ _____

3. Scott ate six pretzels, three cookies, and a brownie. How many snacks did he eat?

_____ snacks

4. Write four number sentences using 6, 9, and 15.

___ + ___ = ___

___ + ___ = ___

___ − ___ = ___

___ − ___ = ___

5. Is it symmetrical?

yes   no

Name the patterns.

_____

_____

_____

Daily Math Practice

Daily Progress Record ⟨27⟩

How many did you get correct each day? Color the squares.

	Monday	Tuesday	Wednesday	Thursday	Friday
5					▓
4					▓
3					
2					
1					

1. $\begin{array}{r} 1\,3 \\ -\ \ 5 \\ \hline \end{array}$

2. 2 4 6 ___ ___ ___

3. $\begin{array}{r} 1\,2 \\ -\ \ 2 \\ \hline \end{array}$

4. Write the number.

nine ___   one ___

six ___   four ___

5. If John eats $\frac{1}{2}$ of his sandwich for lunch and $\frac{1}{2}$ of his sandwich for snack after school, how much is left?

_____

---

1. 6 + 3 + 2 = _____

2. 30 + 40 = _____

3. What comes next?

 ___

4. Tally to show 37.

5. The block tower has four blocks on the base, three blocks on the next two levels, and one block on top. How many blocks are in the tower?

_____ blocks

EMC 750 • © Evan-Moor Corp.

1. $7 + 4 =$ _____

2. $5 + 6 =$ _____

3. Mr. Brown asked 5 students to each bring 2 books they had written to the PTA meeting. How many books did Mr. Brown ask for?

_____ books

4. Write the time.

_____ o'clock

5. $17 + 4 = 21$, so $21 - 4 =$ ___

1. $9 + 5 =$ _____

2. $15 + 0 =$ _____

3. Six cars parked in the first row. Seven cars parked in the second row. Five cars parked in the third row. Which row had the most cars?

_____ row

4. Write a number sentence.

___ ☐ ___ = ___

5. $8 > 6$

yes   no

Friday ⟨28⟩

Super Scoops

 = 1 student

| vanilla | chocolate | mint | cookies 'n cream | butter brickle | strawberry |

How many students like ice cream? _____ students

Which flavor is most popular?_____

Do more students like mint and strawberry together, or vanilla? _____

What is your favorite flavor? _____

Daily Progress Record ⟨28⟩

How many did you get correct each day? Color the squares.

	Monday	Tuesday	Wednesday	Thursday	Friday
5					▓▓▓
4					
3					
2					
1					

1. $6 + 5 =$ _____

2. $14 - 5 =$ _____

3. Sara's window has four corners and four equal sides. What shape is Sara's window?

_____

4. How much?

 and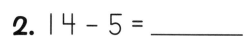

_____ cents

5. Mark the even numbers.

1 2 3 4 5 6 7 8

1. $8 + 7 =$ _____

2.
$$
\begin{array}{r}
11 \\
+\ 3 \\
\hline
\end{array}
$$

3. Write a story problem. $7 - 5 = ?$

_____

_____

_____

4. Tessa has four brothers and two sisters. How many children are in Tessa's family?

○ 6 ○ 5 ○ 7 ○ 8

5. Which is longer?

○ one inch

○ one foot

1. $100 - 10 =$ _____

2. $\begin{array}{r} 10 \\ +\ 6 \\ \hline \end{array}$

3. Carly sold three boxes of candy. Seth sold seven boxes. How many boxes did they sell?

_____ boxes

4. Mark the shapes with more than three sides.

5. Add 10.

2 ___ 4 ___ 5 ___

1. $1,999 + 0 =$ _____

2. $20 + 40 + 10 =$ _____

3. If Tina has ten puppies and four leashes, how many puppies <u>don't</u> have leashes?

_____ puppies

4. Write four number sentences using 13, 7, and 6.

___ + ___ = ___

___ + ___ = ___

___ − ___ = ___

___ − ___ = ___

5. $\begin{array}{r} 8 \\ +\ 9 \\ \hline \end{array}$

Friday 〈29〉

Each group needs two pencils and a ruler.

If Mr. Jones has six groups, how many

pencils does he need to find?

_____ pencils

How many rulers?

_____ rulers

Daily Progress Record 〈29〉

How many did you get correct each day? Color the squares.

	Monday	Tuesday	Wednesday	Thursday	Friday
5					▓
4					▓
3					▓
2					
1					

1. Mark the seventh pin.

2.   4
     + 8
     ____

3. How many different letters are in Stephanie's name?

_____ letters

4. 25 30 35 ___ ___ ___

___ ___ ___

5. 8 + 8 = _____

7 + 7 = _____

6 + 6 = _____

5 + 5 = _____

1. 9 + 2 = _____

2. 6 – 4 = _____

3. Eight coconuts were on the tree. Three fell off. How many are left?

_____ coconuts

4. Write the time.

_____ o'clock

5. Color the beads. Make the spheres green. Make the cubes purple.

1. $17 - 8 =$ _____

2. 5
    5
 + 5
_____

3. Minnie likes even numbers. Mickey likes odd numbers. Who will like 7?

_____

4. Write a number sentence.

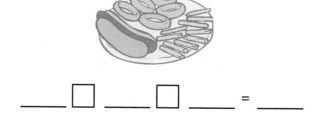

_____ ☐ _____ ☐ _____ = _____

5. 40 pounds is heavier than 30 pounds.

     yes   no

1. $7 + 5 =$ _____

2. $5 - 5 =$ _____

3. There were four plates, four cups, and four forks on the table. Tell how many people you think will eat.

_____ people

4. Write four ways to make 6.

_____

_____

_____

_____

5. $8 + 9 = 17$, so

_____ $= 9 +$ _____

I put six pretzels, four marshmallows,
and two cookies in my snack bag.
How many things do I have in all?

_____ things

If I eat the pretzels, how many
will I have left?

_____ things

Daily Math Practice

Daily Progress Record 30

How many did you get correct each day? Color the squares.

	Monday	Tuesday	Wednesday	Thursday	Friday
5					
4					
3					
2					
1					

94

1. 6 + 4 = _____

2. 5 + 6 = _____

3. Timothy asked for six paper clips. He used two on a puppet and two on a book. How many did he have left?

_____ paper clips

4. Color $\frac{1}{3}$.

5. Draw lines from the words to the correct numbers.

2	five	5
	three	
3	six	6
	four	
4	seven	7
	two	

1.   42
       − 2
    ———

2.   341
       + 23
    ———

3. Seven butterflies flew to four flowers. How many more butterflies than flowers were there?

_____ more butterflies

4. Estimate.

   ○ 1   ○ 10

   ○ 100   ○ 1,000

5. 9 < 9   yes   no

    9 > 9   yes   no

    9 = 9   yes   no

1. 16 – 8 = _____

2. Mark members of the 8 family.

○ 8 + 0   ○ 7 + 2   ○ 5 + 3

3. Sue put six black beads, six brown beads, and a pendant on her necklace. How many beads did she use?

_____ beads

4. Draw lines to name the shapes.

□   ○   △   ▭

triangle square rectangle circle

5. Three girls played on the swings. Four boys played on the monkey bars. Six other children played four square. How many children in all?

○ 3 + 4 = 7

○ 3 + 4 + 6 = 17

○ 4 + 6 = 10

○ 3 + 4 + 6 = 13

---

1. Finish the pattern.

1 3 5 7 ___ ___ ___ ___

2. 4 + 7 + 2 = _____

3. Cathy asked Zack to help her fill the planter box. It needed five bags of soil mix. If Cathy already put in two bags, how many more do they need to put in? _____ more bags

4. 5 + 5 = _____

6 + 6 = _____

7 + 7 = _____

8 + 8 = _____

9 + 9 = _____

5. Is it symmetrical?

yes   no

Friday ⟨31⟩

Color the circles in as many different ways as you can. Color them red or blue. How many ways?

Daily Progress Record ⟨31⟩

How many did you get correct each day? Color the squares.

	Monday	Tuesday	Wednesday	Thursday	Friday
5					
4					
3					
2					
1					

1. $67 - 52 =$ _____

2.
$$\begin{array}{r} 42 \\ 31 \\ +15 \\ \hline \end{array}$$

3. Drew needs a new pair of sweat pants. He has $10. If the pants cost $8, how much change will he get?

$_____

4. $54 + 32 = 86$, so

_____ $- 32 =$ _____

5. Write the time.

half past _____

1. $4 + 2 + 7 + 1 =$ _____

2. $5 + 3 - 2 =$ _____

3. Patrice made cookies for her friends. If she has a dozen and gives them to six friends, how many will each friend get?

_____ cookies

4. Color $\frac{1}{4}$.

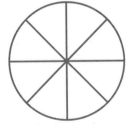

5. Write the number.

one hundred _____

1. $18 - 7 =$ _____

2. $15 + 13 =$ _____

3. 2 4 6 ____ ____ ____

4. $647 < 532$

     yes   no

5. Five frogs each ate five flies. How many flies did the frogs eat?

_____ flies

---

1. $3 + 4 + 9 =$ _____

2. $9 - 2 - 3 =$ _____

3. Mark the rectangles.

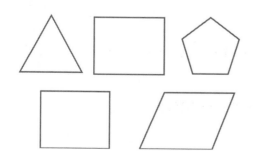

4. Tally to show 48.

5. Cindy had four nickels in her purse and two nickels in her pocket. How many nickels did she have in all?

_____ nickels

What are they worth?

_____ cents

Friday ⟨32⟩

Count the letters in each name: Stephanie, Sam, Susan, Stephan, Scott. Record the information on the graph. Then read the graph and write something that you learned.

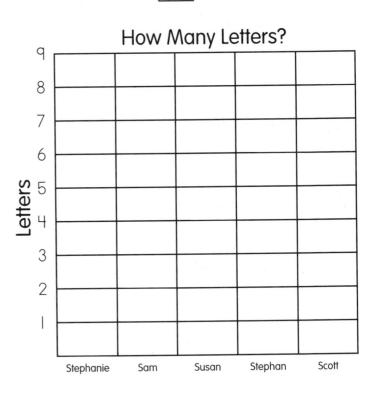

How Many Letters?

Daily Progress Record ⟨32⟩

How many did you get correct each day? Color the squares.

	Monday	Tuesday	Wednesday	Thursday	Friday
5					
4					
3					
2					
1					

1. $5 + 8 =$ _____

2. $14 - 9 =$ _____

3. The fishbowl had 6 guppies, 2 goldfish, 1 catfish, and a snail. How many animals lived in the fishbowl?

_____ animals

4. How much?

 _____ cents

 _____ cents

 _____ cents

5. Think.

$6 + 2 + 1 + 0 =$ _____

---

1. $17 - 8 =$ _____

2. $4 + 6 =$ _____

3. 50 60 70 ___ ___

___ ___ ___

4. Name the pattern.

_____

5. Jesse cut out three hearts, six circles, and three squares. Draw a pattern. Use all the shapes.

1.
$$\begin{array}{r} 8 \\ -\ 2 \\ \hline \end{array}$$

2.
$$\begin{array}{r} 7 \\ 1 \\ +\ 5 \\ \hline \end{array}$$

4. Mark members of the 6 family.

○ 3 + 3   ○ 1 + 6

○ 2 + 5   ○ 4 + 3

○ 5 + 1

5. 84 + 0 = _____

3. Dave found four eggs in the nest and five eggs in the basket. How many eggs did he find?

_____ eggs

1. 8 + 9 = _____

2. 18 − 6 = _____

3. Bev and Jo each picked four flowers. They put three in a vase. How many flowers are left?

_____ flowers

4. Mark the figures with four corners and four sides.

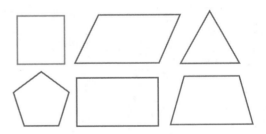

5. 32 is an odd number.

yes   no

Friday ⟨33⟩

Solve this problem.

$$20 + 20 + 20 - 10 + 1 = \_\_\_\_\_$$

Great Job!

Daily Progress Record ⟨33⟩

How many did you get correct each day? Color the squares.

	Monday	Tuesday	Wednesday	Thursday	Friday
5					
4					
3					
2					
1					

Monday 34

1. $\begin{array}{r} 52 \\ -41 \\ \hline \end{array}$

2. $\begin{array}{r} 37 \\ +41 \\ \hline \end{array}$

3. Erik ate five pieces of pizza. If the pizza was cut into eight pieces, how many are left?

_____ pieces

4. Mark the tenth balloon.

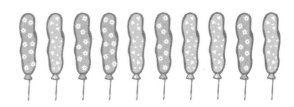

5. 5 10 15 ____ ____ ____

____ ____ ____ ____

Tuesday 34

1. Two pounds is more than $\frac{1}{2}$ pound.   yes   no

2. $\begin{array}{r} 73 \\ 14 \\ +12 \\ \hline \end{array}$

3. If six kids each make two piles of sand, how many piles of sand are there in all? _____ piles

4. $10 + 2 = ?$

○ $4 + 8$ ○ $7 + 3$

○ $11 + 0$ ○ $9 + 3$

5. Circle the clock that shows 6:30.

 6:00   12:30   6:30

Wednesday 34

1. $943 - 0 = $ _____

2. Mark the even numbers.

   3 8 1 6 4 2 9

3. $7 + 10 = $ _____ .
   $6 + 10 = $ _____
   $5 + 10 = $ _____

4. Twenty-six first-graders went to the dairy. If the bus holds fourteen students, how many buses will they need?

   _____ buses

   How many extra seats?

   _____ seats

5. How much?

   7 🪙 s = _____ cents

Thursday 34

1. $8 + 2 + 5 + 3 = $ _____

2. $25 + 34 = 59$, so
   ___ $- 34 = $ ___

3. $9 - 9 = $ _____
   $8 - 8 = $ _____
   $7 - 7 = $ _____

4. Ronni rode her bike to Joe's house. If Joe's house is eight blocks away, how many blocks did she ride by the time she got home?

   _____ blocks

5. Write a number sentence to show how many legs there are.

   ___ + ___ + ___ + ___ = ___

Friday 34

Finish the graph. Make a square for each book.

		The Books We Read
Animal books	— ‖‖ ///	
Fairy tales	— ‖‖ //	
Sports books	— //	
Chapter books	— ////	
Holiday books	— ‖‖	

The Books We Read

Animal books	
Fairy tales	
Sports books	
Chapter books	
Holiday books	

Read the graph. Write something you learned.

☐ = 1 book

Daily Progress Record 34

How many did you get correct each day? Color the squares.

	Monday	Tuesday	Wednesday	Thursday	Friday
5					
4					
3					
2					
1					

1. $4 + 5 + 3 + 0 =$ _____

2. Is it symmetrical?

   yes   no

3. If Timmy pops three balloons, how many balloons will be left?

_____ balloons

4. $11 + 10 =$ _____

$12 + 10 =$ _____

$13 + 10 =$ _____

$14 + 10 =$ _____

$15 + 10 =$ _____

5. 10 20 30 ____ ____

____ ____ ____ ____ ____

1. $17 - 8 =$ _____

2. $8 + 1 + 4 =$ _____

3. There are five eggs in the last row, four eggs in the fourth row, three eggs in the third row, two eggs in the second row, and one egg in the first row. How many eggs are in the egg pyramid? _____ eggs

4. $64 - 33 = 31$, so

____ $- 31 =$ ____

5. Write a number sentence.

____ ☐ ____ = ____

1. $5 + 2 + 7 =$ _____

2. $38 - 34 =$ _____

3. Bo made 4 baskets. If he gets two points for each basket, how many points did he make?

_____ points

4. Finish the pattern.

___ ___ ___ ___

5. Estimate.

○ exactly 30
○ more than 30
○ less than 30

---

1. $62 + 37 =$ _____

2. $19 - 8 =$ _____

3. How many sides are there on two squares?

_____ sides

4. 90 80 70

___ ___ ___ ___ ___

5. Write the number words.

1 _____

2 _____

3 _____

4 _____

5 _____

Friday 35

Draw each shape in a different box.

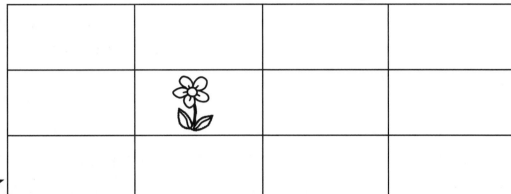

Write directions to each shape. Always start at the star.
The first one has been done for you.

　Go right 2 boxes. Go up 1 box.

♡　_____

◯　_____

Daily Progress Record ⟨35⟩

How many did you get correct each day? Color the squares.

	Monday	Tuesday	Wednesday	Thursday	Friday
5					▓
4					▓
3					▓
2					
1					

1. $325 - 214 =$ _____

2. Color $\frac{1}{4}$.

3. Sammy has two trucks, seven cars, and an ambulance. How many vehicles does he have?

_____ vehicles

4. Fill in the correct symbol.

$<$ $=$ $>$

$8 \square 6$ $8 \square 8$ $8 \square 9$

5. Write the time.

_____ o'clock

1. $47 + 22 =$ _____

2.
$$\begin{array}{r} 5 \\ 10 \\ 4 \\ + \ 10 \\ \hline \end{array}$$

3. $1 + 0, 2 + 0, 3 + 0,$

_____, _____,

_____, _____

4. Tally to show 84.

5. There are twenty parking spaces in the lot. If fifteen cars are parked, how many spaces are empty?

_____ spaces

1. $89 - 34 =$ _____

2. $73 + 15 =$ _____

3. Six friends came to Helen's store. They each brought one dollar. How much money did they bring in all?

$_____

4. 2 ___ 6 ___
10 ___ 14 ___

5. Write the numbers.

eleven _____

fourteen _____

nineteen _____

twelve _____

1. $24 + 43 =$ _____

2. $38 - 6 =$ _____

3. How many more eggs does Joy need to fill her carton if she has seven eggs now?

 _____ more eggs

4. Finish the pattern.

___ ___ ___ ___ ___

5. Mark the clock that shows the same time.

[6:00] [3:00] [12:00]

Friday 36

Josh wanted to sort his Legos®.

He had six different shapes.

Tell a way that Josh could sort

them into two groups, and draw

to show what shapes would go in

each group.

Daily Math Practice

Daily Progress Record 36

How many did you get correct each day? Color the squares.

	Monday	Tuesday	Wednesday	Thursday	Friday
5					
4					
3					
2					
1					

How to Solve
Word Problems

 Read the problem carefully. Think about what it says.

 Look for clue words. The clue words will tell you if you should add or subtract.

 Solve the problem.

 Check your work. Make sure your answer makes sense.

Clue Words

Add	Subtract
in all	more than
altogether	less than
total	are left
sum	take away
both	difference
plus	fewer

Week 1

Monday
1. 4
2. 6
3. 2 balls
4. 4 cents
5. 5, 4, 3, 2, 1, 0

Tuesday
1. 7
2. 8
3. three
4. The circles should be colored.
5. 2 + 2 = 4

Wednesday
1. 5
2. 2
3. 5 pets
4. 3 + 1 = 4, 1 + 3 = 4
5. ABAB

Thursday
1. 10
2. 3
3. 8
4. 4, 7, 9, 2, 0, 6, and 3 should be circled.
5. 2 dolls

Friday
Answers will vary.

Week 2

Monday
1. big dog
2. 4
3. The first star should be colored.
4. 6
5. 6 cents

Tuesday
1. 8
2. 3
3. yes
4. no
5. 6 bikes

Wednesday
1. 9
2. 5
3. All but the tricycle should be colored.
4. 8 o'clock
5. 15, 20, 25

Thursday
1. 10
2. 7
3. 3 + 2 = 5
4. 4 shoes
5. circle

Friday
swings 4, balls 8, ropes 3, climbing bars 5 balls

Week 3

Monday
1. 8
2. 7
3. 1, 2, 3
4. two balls = two balls, one ball = one ball
5. 2 bones

Tuesday
1. 6
2. 4 sides, 4 corners
3. 4 cookies
4. 10
5. 2 + 4 = 4 + 2

Wednesday
1. 5
2. 3
3. 12
4. 1 bird
5. 10, 20, 30

Thursday
1. One-half of the ball should be colored.
2. 3 + 3 = 6
3. 11
4. 9
5. 4 cars

Friday
Patterns will vary. Students can tell about their patterns orally or in writing (e.g., "My pattern is red, blue, blue," or "My pattern is ABB.").

Week 4

Monday
1. 9
2. 6
3. block
4.
5. 4

Tuesday
1. 8
2. 10
3. 6 kittens
4. 8 o'clock
5. 6, 7, 8, 9

Wednesday
1. 7
2. 11
3. blue square, red circle, yellow triangle
4. $0 + 2 = 2$, $2 - 2 = 0$
5. 5 hats

Thursday
1. 9
2. 12
3. 6 beads
4. $2 + 5 = 7$
5. no, yes, yes

Friday
Groups will vary.

Week 5

Monday
1. 4
2. 6
3. 6
4. 7 cents
5. 5 stamps

Tuesday
1. 6
2. 8
3. 10, 9, 8, 7, 6, 5, 4, 3, 2, 1, 0
4. yes, yes, no
5. 7 things

Wednesday
1. 6
2. 10, 6, 4
3. 9
4. AABAAB, triangle
5. $4 + 6 = 10$ cookies

Thursday
1. 10, 11, 12, 13, 14, 15, 16
2. 3
3. Mr. Brown
4. 5
5. yes, yes, no

Friday
The balls should be numbered in order from smallest to largest or largest to smallest.

Week 6

Monday
1. 3
2. 7
3. 5 pennies
4. 10 o'clock
5. The second hat should be marked.

Tuesday
1. 6
2. 0
3. drawing of triangle—3 sides, 3 corners
4. The side with two should be marked.
5. 3 stamps

Wednesday
1. 5
2. 8
3. 5, 10, 15, 20
4. The two square buttons with two holes should be marked.
5. 7 fish

Thursday
1. 4
2. 9
3. 2 pages
4. $3 + 2 = 5$
5. 3

Friday
6 birds, 3 cages

EMC 750 • © Evan-Moor Corp.

Week 7

Monday
1. 2
2. 9
3. 4 eggs
4. The half banana should be marked.
5. Answers will vary.

Tuesday
1. 5
2. 7
3. yes, no, no
4. dark square, light square, dark square, light square
5. 6 beads

Wednesday
1. 0
2. 7
3. 20
4. yes, no
5. 10 + 10 = 20

Thursday
1. 6
2. 4
3. 10, 5, 7
4. The squares should be marked.
5. 6 feathers

Friday

3 rainy days, 4 cloudy days, yes
Additional information will vary.

Week 8

Monday
1. 10
2. 2
3. 6 cups
4. 1 ten 4 ones
5. circle, triangle

Tuesday
1. 4
2. 9
3. 3 frogs
4. 9:00
5. 2 + 3 + 4 = 9

Wednesday
1. 20
2. 5
3. 10
4. 2, 4, 6, 8, 10
5. yes, no, no

Thursday
1. 3
2. 1
3. 26 students
4. The triangles should be marked.
5. 2 + 2 = 4

Friday
12 ears , 16 feet, 3 tails

Week 9

Monday
1. 4
2. 10
3. 12 pieces
4. yes
5. 8 cents

Tuesday
1. 3
2. 9
3. 4
4. 18, 17, 16, 15, 14, 13
5. 3 tens

Wednesday
1. 8
2. 3
3. 7 pockets
4. yes, no, yes, yes
5. no

Thursday
1. 6
2. 9
3. Todd, 1
4. ABBABB
5. 322

Friday
Patterns will vary.

Week 10

Monday
1. 10
2. 9
3. 4 pumpkins
4. The third bird should be marked.
5. yes, yes, yes, no

Tuesday
1. 3
2. 11
3. 8 pennies
4. The second and fourth hats should be marked.
5. 6 o'clock

Wednesday
1. 11
2. 6
3. Sue
4. 5, 10, 15, 20
5. 3 half-gallons of milk

Thursday
1. 1
2. 2
3. 5 cents
4. The squares should be marked.
5. 9 pieces of fruit

Friday
12

Week 11

Monday
1. 9
2. 5
3. 8 tortillas
4. 8, 6, 3, 0
5. 40

Tuesday
1. 11
2. 8
3. 10
4. One section of the square should be colored.
5. yes, no

Wednesday
1. 9
2. 8
3. no, no, yes
4. 1 + 2 = 3
5. 11 members

Thursday
1. 48
2. 12
3. 9 bears
4. 24
5. 4 + 2 = 6, 2 + 4 = 6, 6 − 2 = 4, 6 − 4 = 2

Friday
17 teeth, September, October
Additional responses will vary.

Week 12

Monday
1. 7
2. 3
3. 16 oranges
4. 11 o'clock
5.

Tuesday
1. 12
2. 50
3. 6 raisins
4. 221221
5. 2, 4, 6, 8, 10

Wednesday
1. 8
2. 55
3. 12 peanuts
4. The ball and marble should be marked.
5. 5 + 2 = 7, 7 − 2 = 5

Thursday
1. 10
2. 6
3. 10 books
4. 7, 6, 10, 2
5. One section of the circle should be colored.

Friday
14 pieces of fruit

EMC 750 • © Evan-Moor Corp.

Week 13

Monday
1. 0
2. 10
3. 4 blocks
4. aabaab
5. 40 cents

Tuesday
1. 15
2. 11
3. 7
4. The circles should be marked.
5. 8 pieces

Wednesday
1. 10
2. 1
3. yes, yes, no
4. Sentences will vary.
5. Problems will vary.

Thursday
1. 6
2. 2
3. 5 treats
4. even, odd, even
5. 5 + 2, 6 + 1, 9 − 2, 7 + 0

Friday
$20

Week 14

Monday
1. 12
2. 5
3. 10 cents
4. The seventh bird should be marked.
5. 20, 25

Tuesday
1. 7
2. 11
3. 100 pounds
4. 9 o'clock
5. 4 other flowers

Wednesday
1. 11
2. 11
3. 9 pieces
4. 4 sides, 4 corners
5. yes, no, yes

Thursday
1. 2
2. 12
3. 10 ants
4. 3 + 6, 4 + 5, 2 + 7, 0 + 9
5. 30 cents

Friday
10 toes, 20 toes, 30 toes, 50 toes

Week 15

Monday
1. 12
2. 7
3. 6 fish
4. yes, no
5. striped, dotted

Tuesday
1. 13
2. 0
3. 7 cookies
4. The first pizza should be marked.
5. ten

Wednesday
1. 12
2. 7
3. 6 bones
4. 50
5. no

Thursday
1. 13
2. 9
3. 10
4. 3 + 5 = 8, 5 + 3 = 8, 8 − 3 = 5, 8 − 5 = 3
5. no

Friday
4; 1; no, 2 + 1 = 3; yes

Week ⟨16⟩

Monday
1. 14
2. 14
3. 5 years older
4. The second pie should be marked.
5. 8

Tuesday
1. 14
2. 0
3. 10 laps
4. rectangle, triangle, circle
5. ⵜⵜⵜ ⵜⵜⵜ /

Wednesday
1. 1
2. 12
3. 9 pencils
4. 53
5. three

Thursday
1. 15
2. 8
3. 7 hits
4. 10 o'clock
5. The big square should be marked.

Friday
6 books

Week ⟨17⟩

Monday
1. 15
2. 11
3. 8 bears
4. 32, 31, 30, 29, 28, 27, 26, 25
5. 6 + 5 = 11, 5 + 6 = 11, 11 – 5 = 6, 11 – 6 = 5

Tuesday
1. 15
2. 14
3. 10 drumsticks
4. 9
5. Sentences will vary. Sue saw seven fish swimming in the lake—two gray fish and five white fish.

Wednesday
1. 16
2. 7
3. 0 cupcakes
4. 40, 50, 60, 70, 80, 90, 100
5. 3, 4, 5

Thursday
1. 13
2. 12
3. 10 things
4. Group 1 has flowers with four petals.
   Group 2 has flowers with five petals.
5. 7

Friday
Answers will vary.

Week ⟨18⟩

Monday
1. 16
2. 15
3. 20 grams
4. The seventh bead should be marked.
5. 3 pink hearts

Tuesday
1. 10
2. 17
3.
4. 4 o'clock
5. 5 friends

Wednesday
1. 17
2. 15
3. $2
4. 1 – 1 = 0
5. 5, 10, 15, 20, 25, 30, 35, 40

Thursday
1. 14
2. 1
3. 1 more
4. 4 sides, 3 sides
5. 3 + 2, 6 – 1, 5 + 0

Friday
14 squares

Monday
1. 18
2. 3
3. 3 girls
4. 36
5. One piece of the rectangle should be colored.

Tuesday
1. 11
2. 2
3. 18 bulbs
4. Stories will vary.
5. 30

Wednesday
1. 13
2. 8
3. 0 more
4. no, yes, no
5. 10 pounds

Thursday
1. 7
2. 5
3. 8 books
4. red, yellow, yellow, red, red
5. yes

Friday
dog, snake, cat and bird
Additional responses will vary.

Monday
1. 1
2. 16
3. 30 candies
4. Two pieces of the pie should be colored.
5. one, two, three, four

Tuesday
1. 12
2. 3
3. circle, triangle, triangle
4. 卌 卌 ////
5. 9 passengers

Wednesday
1. 11
2. 2
3. 30 blocks
4. 2, 4, 6, 8, 10, 12, 14, 16
5. The cone should be marked.

Thursday
1. 104
2. 8
3. 3 hats
4. 3 o'clock
5. 30

Friday
11 times

Monday
1. 17
2. 1
3. 5 bags
4. Three closed figures should be marked.
5. 6 + 2 = 8, 2 + 6 = 8, 8 − 6 = 2, 8 − 2 = 6

Tuesday
1. 13
2. 13
3. 8 blocks
4. AABBAABB
5. 10, 20, 30, 40, 50

Wednesday
1. 647
2. 13
3. The first one should be marked.
4. 10 − 3 = 7
5. 3 + 4 + 1 = 8 pieces

Thursday
1. 17
2. 4
3. 8 wheels
4. 30 cents
5. yes

Friday
2 packages

Week 22

Monday
1. 0
2. 11 balls
3. 11, 12, 13
4. 2 o'clock
5. The basket should be marked.

Tuesday
1. 12
2. 2
3. 2 days
4. 7
5. 20, 25, 30, 35, 40, 45, 50, 55, 60

Wednesday
1. 16
2. 0
3. 5 trees
4. 25 cents
5. 5 + 3, 4 + 4, 8 + 0

Thursday
1. 14
2. $.50 or 50 cents or 50¢
3. yes
4. 10, 9, 8, 7, 6
5. Four straight lines should be marked.

Friday
The first drawing should be marked.

Week 23

Monday
1. 18
2. 8
3. 9 eggs
4. Three pigs should be colored.
5. 0, 4, 8, 2

Tuesday
1. 13
2. 14 bones
3. The heart should be divided symmetrically.
4. 2 tens + 3 ones = 23 in all
5. three, five, seven

Wednesday
1. 16
2. 4
3. 10 children
4. mitten, hat
5. The rectangles should be marked.

Thursday
1. 9
2. 13
3. 6 jelly beans
4. 19, 20
5. 2 + 6 = 8, 6 + 2 = 8, 8 − 2 = 6, 8 − 6 = 2

Friday

1.

2.

3.

4.

Week 24

Monday
1. 11
2. 6
3. yes
4. Two marbles should be colored.
5. 12 legs

Tuesday
1. 17
2. 9
3. 4 more crates
4. ///// ///// ///// /

5.

one more	one less	ten more	ten less
41 _42_	_20_ 21	6 _16_	_29_ 39
86 _87_	_53_ 54	30 _40_	_87_ 97

Wednesday
1. 17
2. 5
3. 29 drawing tools
4. 1 o'clock
5. 5

Thursday
1. 14
2. 3
3. 3 flies
4. no
5. 0, 3, 0

Friday
Group 1 – 3, Group 2 – 8,
Group 3 – 5, Group 4 – 9,
Group 5 – 7, Group 6 – 4,
Group 7 – 8, Group 8 – 6,
Group 9 – 5, Group 10 – 10

EMC 750 • © Evan-Moor Corp.

Week 25

Monday
1. 4
2. 8 nails
3. 11
4. 35 cents
5. 62, 61, 60, 59, 58, 57

Tuesday
1. 5
2. AABCAABC
3. 28
4. The circles should be marked.
5. 19 books

Wednesday
1. 10
2. 9
3. 8,247
4. 2 + 1 = 3
5. no

Thursday
1. 8
2. 17
3. 10 things
4. Stories will vary.
5. 4 centimeters

Friday
The banana should be marked. Answers will vary but should indicate that all are things you can sit on, or are pieces of furniture.

Week 26

Monday
1. 19
2. 8
3. 14 flags
4. The second star should be marked.
5. 20, 25, 30, 35, 40, 45, 50

Tuesday
1. 13
2. 15
3. 12 sandwiches
4. The gallon of milk should be marked.
5. Group A: < (less than 7)
   Group B: > (more than 7)

Wednesday
1. 9
2. 49, 49
3. 9 rungs
4. 12, 13, 14
5. pink square, green circle, black triangle

Thursday
1. 9
2. 19
3.
4. 5 + 7 = 12
5. 8 + 1, 3 + 6, 5 + 4

Friday
11 goals in all, at least three goals

Week 27

Monday
1. 12
2. 14
3. 16 cars
4. right 2 boxes
5. ten, five, seven

Tuesday
1. 10
2. 5
3. 11 bugs
4. yes
5. 6

Wednesday
1. 15
2. 10
3. 2 cookies
4. Stories will vary.
5. 21 + 23 or any other two-number combination that equals 44

Thursday
1. 15
2. 9
3. 10 snacks
4. 6 + 9 = 15, 9 + 6 = 15, 15 − 6 = 9, 15 − 9 = 6
5. no

Friday
ABAB, AABAAB, ABCABC

Week 28

Monday
1. 8
2. 8, 10, 12
3. 10
4. 9, 1, 6, 4
5. none

Tuesday
1. 11
2. 70
3. triangle
4.
5. 11 blocks

Wednesday
1. 11
2. 11
3. 10 books
4. 5 o'clock
5. 17

Thursday
1. 14
2. 15
3. second row
4. Answers will vary.
5. yes

Friday
19 students, cookies 'n cream, vanilla—Two more like vanilla. Answers will vary.

Week 29

Monday
1. 11
2. 9
3. square
4. 16 cents
5. 2, 4, 6, 8

Tuesday
1. 15
2. 14
3. Stories will vary.
4. 7 children
5. one foot

Wednesday
1. 90
2. 16
3. 10 boxes
4. All but the triangle should be marked.
5. 12, 14, 15

Thursday
1. 1999
2. 70
3. 6 puppies
4. 7 + 6 = 13, 6 + 7 = 13, 13 − 6 = 7, 13 − 7 = 6
5. 17

Friday
12 pencils, 6 rulers

Week 30

Monday
1. The seventh pin should be marked.
2. 12
3. 8 letters
4. 40, 45, 50, 55, 60, 65
5. 16, 14, 12, 10

Tuesday
1. 11
2. 2
3. 5 coconuts
4. 6 o'clock
5. purple, purple, green, green, purple, purple, green, green

Wednesday
1. 9
2. 15
3. Mickey
4. Answers will vary.
5. yes

Thursday
1. 12
2. 0
3. 4 people
4. Answers will vary.
5. 17 = 9 + 8

Friday
12 things, 6 things

Week 31

Monday
1. 10
2. 11
3. 2 paper clips
4. Two objects should be colored.
5. Lines should correctly connect the numerals and the words.

Tuesday
1. 40
2. 364
3. 3 more butterflies
4. 100
5. no, no, yes

Wednesday
1. 8
2. 8 + 0, 5 + 3
3. 12 beads
4. Lines should correctly connect the shapes and the word names.
5. 3 + 4 + 6 = 13

Thursday
1. 9, 11, 13, 15
2. 13
3. 3 more bags
4. 10, 12, 14, 16, 18
5. no

Friday
(8 ways)
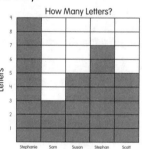

Week 32

Monday
1. 15
2. 88
3. $2
4. 86 – 32 = 54
5. half past 7

Tuesday
1. 14
2. 6
3. 2 cookies
4. Two of the circle's sections should be colored.
5. 100

Wednesday
1. 11
2. 28
3. 8, 10, 12
4. no
5. 25 flies

Thursday
1. 16
2. 4
3. The rectangles should be marked.
4. 𝍷𝍷𝍷𝍷 𝍷𝍷𝍷𝍷 𝍷𝍷𝍷𝍷 𝍷𝍷𝍷𝍷 𝍷𝍷𝍷𝍷 𝍷𝍷𝍷𝍷 𝍷𝍷𝍷𝍷 𝍷𝍷𝍷𝍷 𝍷𝍷𝍷𝍷 𝍷𝍷
5. 6 nickels, 30 cents

Friday
Additional responses will vary.

How Many Letters?

Week 33

Monday
1. 13
2. 5
3. 10 animals
4. 40 cents, 20 cents, 4 cents
5. 9

Tuesday
1. 9
2. 10
3. 80, 90, 100, 110, 120
4. ABACABAC
5. Patterns will vary.

Wednesday
1. 6
2. 13
3. 9 eggs
4. 3 + 3, 5 + 1
5. 84

Thursday
1. 17
2. 12
3. 5 flowers
4. All but the triangle and pentagon should be marked.
5. no

Friday
51

Week 34

Monday
1. 11
2. 78
3. 3 pieces
4. The tenth balloon should be marked.
5. 20, 25, 30, 35, 40, 45, 50

Tuesday
1. yes
2. 99
3. 12 piles
4. 4 + 8, 9 + 3
5.

Wednesday
1. 943
2. 8, 6, 4, 2
3. 17, 16, 15
4. 2 buses, 2 extra seats
5. 35 cents

Thursday
1. 18
2. 59 – 34 = 25
3. 0, 0, 0
4. 16 blocks
5. 6 + 6 + 6 + 6 = 24

Friday
Additional responses
will vary.

The Books We Read

Animal books	☐☐☐☐☐☐☐
Fairy Tales	☐☐☐☐☐☐
Sports books	☐☐
Chapter books	☐☐☐☐☐
Holiday books	☐☐☐☐☐☐

Week 35

Monday
1. 12
2. no
3. 6 balloons
4. 21, 22, 23, 24, 25
5. 40, 50, 60, 70, 80, 90, 100

Tuesday
1. 9
2. 13
3. 15 eggs
4. 64 – 31 = 33
5. Number sentences will vary.

Wednesday
1. 14
2. 4
3. 8 points
4. circle, square, circle, circle
5. more than 30

Thursday
1. 99
2. 11
3. 8 sides
4. 60, 50, 40, 30, 20
5. one, two, three, four, five

Friday
Answers will vary.

Week 36

Monday
1. 111
2. 1/4 of the square should be colored.
3. 10 vehicles
4. 8 > 6, 8 = 8, 8 < 9
5. 4 o'clock

Tuesday
1. 69
2. 29
3. 4 + 0, 5 + 0, 6 + 0, 7 + 0
4. ||||| ||||| ||||| ||||| ||||| ||||| ||||| ||||| |||||
   ||||| ||||| ||||| ||||| ||||| ||||| ||||| ||||| ///
5. 5 spaces

Wednesday
1. 55
2. 88
3. $6
4. 2, 4, 6, 8, 10, 12, 14, 16
5. 11, 14, 19, 12

Thursday
1. 67
2. 32
3. 5 more eggs
4. triangle, inverted triangle, triangle,
   inverted triangle
5. The first clock should be marked.

Friday
Answers will vary.